SEASONAL SUNDAY SOLOS

FOR PIANO

CHRISTMAS, HOLY WEEK, PENTECOST, THANKSGIVING & MORE

ISBN 978-1-4234-7522-4

HAL•LEONARD®
CORPORATION
7777 W. BLUEMOUND RD. P.O. BOX 13819 MILWAUKEE, WI 53213

Visit Hal Leonard Online at
www.halleonard.com

CONTENTS

ALPHABETICAL LISTING OF SONGS

COME, THOU LONG-EXPECTED JESUS

5

Words by CHARLES WESLEY
Music by ROWLAND HUGH PRICHARD

Flowing gently

With pedal

p

cresc.

7

BREATH OF HEAVEN
(Mary's Song)

Words and Music by AMY GRANT
and CHRIS EATON

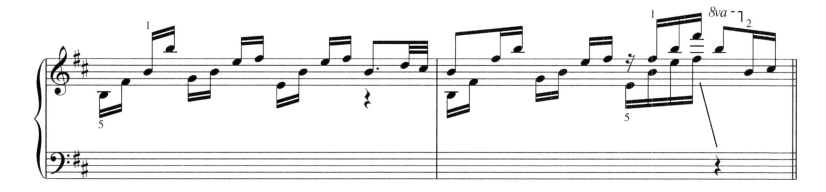

IMMANUEL

Words and Music by
MICHAEL CARD

Warmly

mp

With pedal

DO YOU HEAR WHAT I HEAR

Words and Music by NOEL REGNEY
and GLORIA SHAYNE

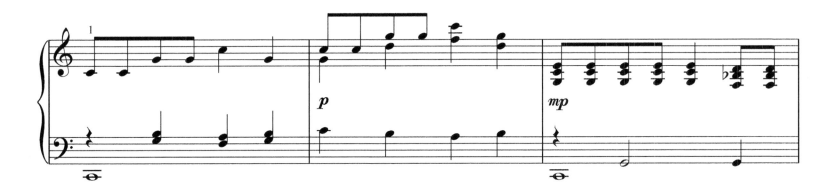

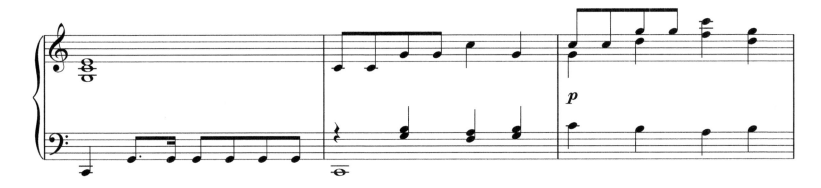

MARY, DID YOU KNOW?

Words and Music by MARK LOWRY
and BUDDY GREENE

Slowly, in 2

WE THREE KINGS OF ORIENT ARE

Words and Music by
JOHN H. HOPKINS, JR.

Steadily, with mystery

To Coda ⊕

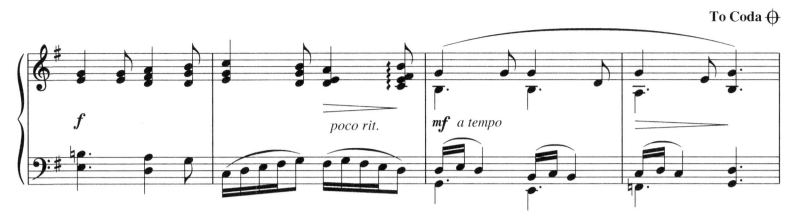

D.S. al Coda

ALL GLORY, LAUD AND HONOR

Words by THEODULPH OF ORLEANS
Translated by JOHN MASON NEALE
Music by MELCHIOR TESCHNER

Majestically

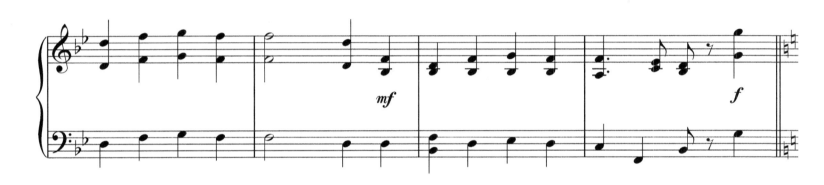

HOSANNA, LOUD HOSANNA

Words by Jenette Threlfall, based on Matthew 21:1-11
Music taken from *Gesangbuch der Herzogl*

Triumphantly

With pedal

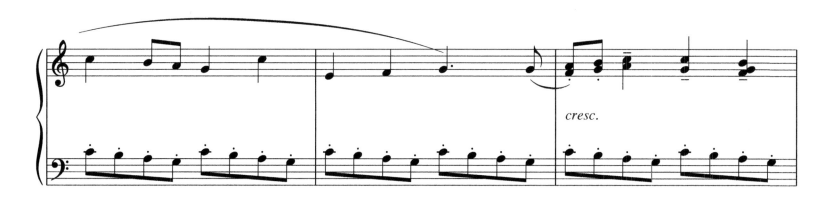

IN THE NAME OF THE LORD

Words by GLORIA GAITHER,
PHILL McHUGH and SANDI PATTY
Music by SANDI PATTY

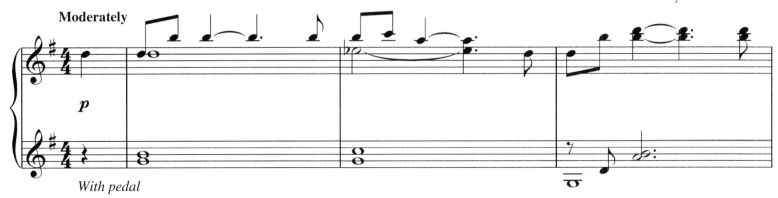

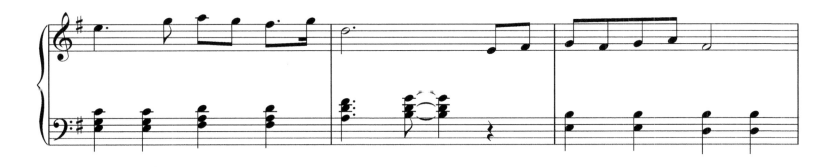

ABOVE ALL

Words and Music by PAUL BALOCHE
and LENNY LeBLANC

Pensively

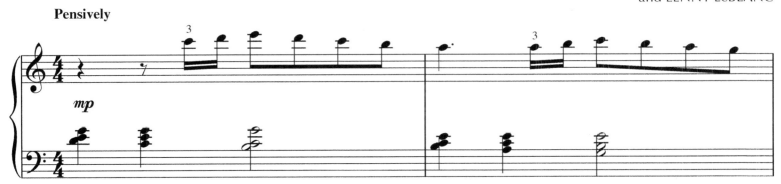

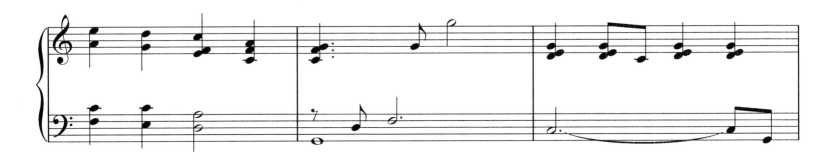

THE WONDERFUL CROSS

Words and Music by JESSE REEVES,
CHRIS TOMLIN and J.D. WALT

O SACRED HEAD, NOW WOUNDED

Words by BERNARD OF CLAIRVAUX
Music by HANS HASSLER

Slowly

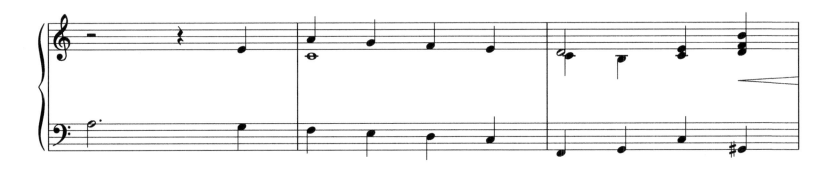

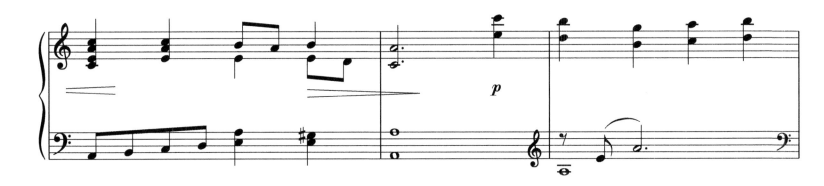

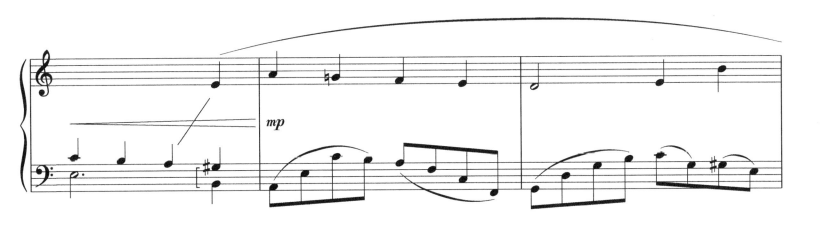

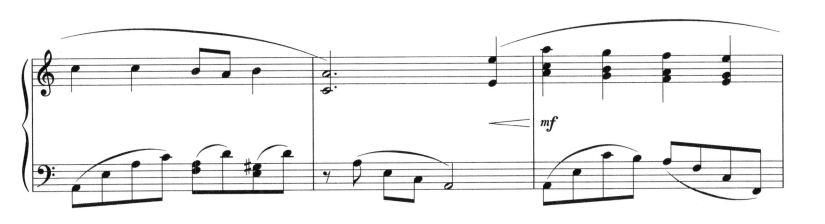

CHRIST THE LORD IS RISEN TODAY

Words by CHARLES WESLEY
Music adapted from *Lyra Davidica*

Allegro

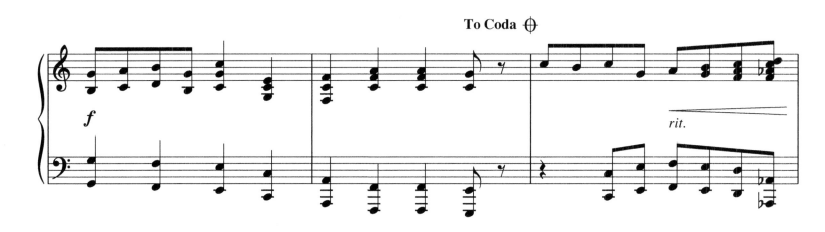

To Coda ⊕

rit.

a tempo
mp *cresc.*

8vb

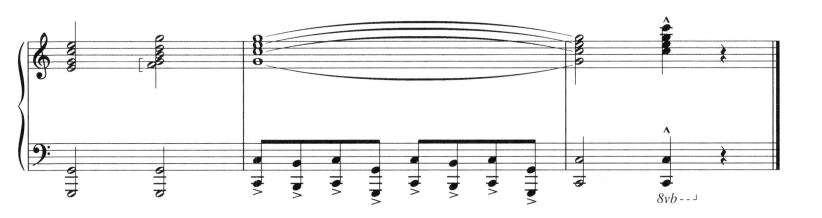

THINE IS THE GLORY

Words by EDMOND LOUIS BUDRY
Music by GEORGE FRIDERIC HANDEL

With energy

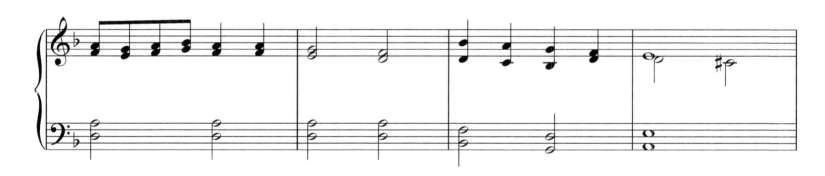

MIGHTY TO SAVE

Words and Music by BEN FIELDING
and REUBEN MORGAN

With praise

CONSUMING FIRE

Words and Music by
TIM HUGHES

Moderately slow

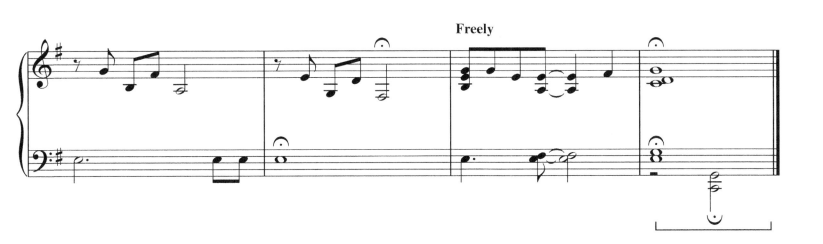

HOLY SPIRIT RAIN DOWN

Words and Music by
RUSSELL FRAGAR

Prayerfully

222

SPIRIT OF THE LIVING GOD

Words and Music by DANIEL IVERSON
and LOWELL ALEXANDER

BATTLE HYMN OF THE REPUBLIC

Words by JULIA WARD HOWE
Music by WILLIAM STEFFE

March tempo, in 2

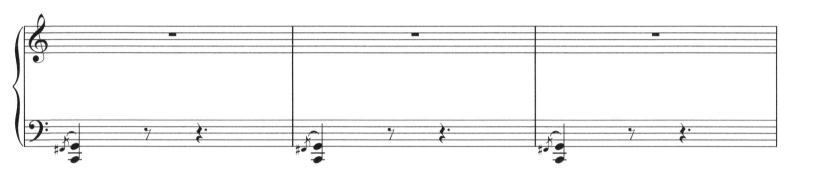

AMERICA, THE BEAUTIFUL

Words by KATHERINE LEE BATES
Music by SAMUEL A. WARD

Freely and slowly, like the calm after a storm

With courage

mf

Triumphantly

rit.

sim.

GOD OF OUR FATHERS

Words by DANIEL CRANE ROBERTS
Music by GEORGE WILLIAM WARREN

Majestically

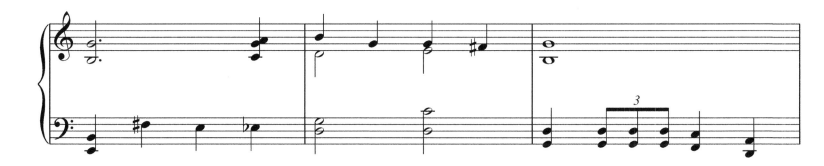

COME, YE THANKFUL PEOPLE, COME

Words by HENRY ALFORD
Music by GEORGE JOB ELVEY

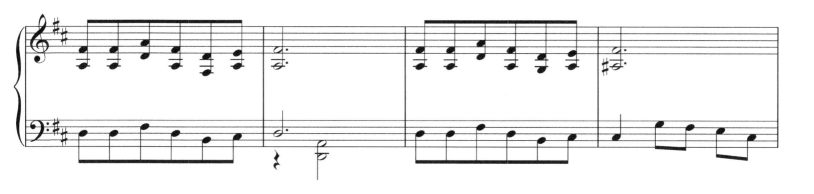

94

WORTHY IS THE LAMB

Words and Music by
DARLENE ZSCHECH

Worshipfully

With pedal

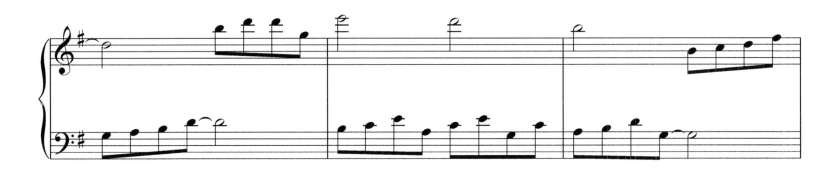

NOW THANK WE ALL OUR GOD

German Words by MARTIN RINKART
English Translation by CATHERINE WINKWORTH
Music by JOHANN CRÜGER

Stately

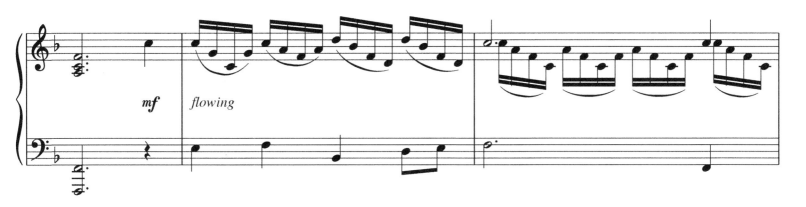

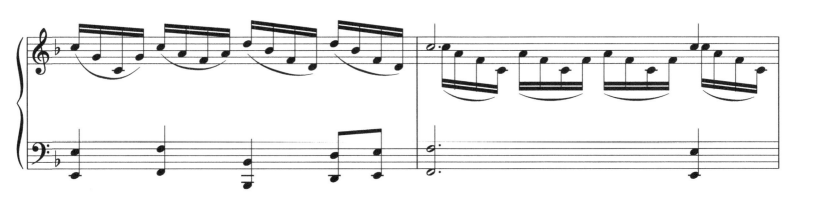

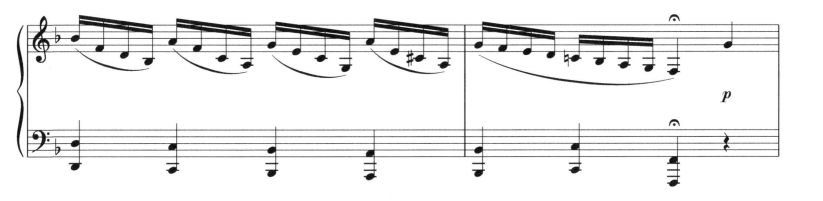

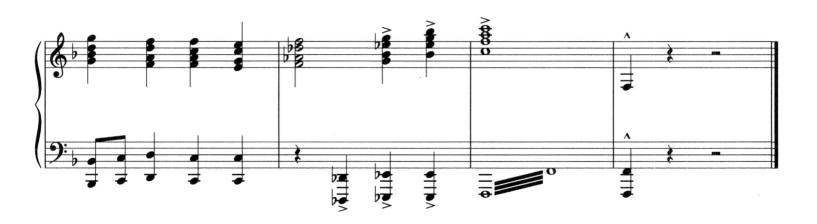